Hope comma Lucent
(You Edify Me)

Poetry/Prosetry

Honey Novick

AF508960

Copyright© 2021 Honey Novick
ISBN: 978-81-8253-754-5

First Edition: 2021
Rs. 200/-

Cyberwit.net
HIG 45 Kaushambi Kunj, Kalindipuram
Allahabad - 211011 (U.P.) India
http://www.cyberwit.net
Tel: +(91) 9415091004
E-mail: info@cyberwit.net

No part of this book may be reproduced or transmitted in any form or by any means, electronic, mechanical, photocopying, or otherwise, without the express written consent of Honey Novick.

Printed at Repro India Limited.

Honey, Dear Honey
(dedication poem by Joan Sutcliffe)

FOREWORD

The 13th century Japanese sage, Nichiren, says, "...fortune comes from 10,000 miles away". When Dr. Agarwal contacted me here, in Toronto, to submit 50 or 60 pieces of my work, I felt as if the words of Nichiren were prescient. In lieu of a bio, I have added a tribute to me, by master poet, Joan Sutcliffe. I hope you enjoy reading this labor of love.

Poet, songwriter, prima donna of the literary salons

and – feminist – par excellence!
Famous in herself
with panoramic sweep of mind
and largesse of heart
she has moved with the greatest
performed before Prime Minister Pierre Trudeau
befriended the tragic young star Sal Mineo
with a book to prove it
opened a conference of leaders in Japan
by vocalization of a moving peace chant.
this is Honey – yes, her real name
like Madhu in Hindi
or Mielita in Spanish
sweet as honey, but dynamic as a spinning top
taking flight above the clouds
proud as a peacock
yet the humble worshipper at the shrine of true art.
She is the innovator of new ideas
and like all who give birth to the out-of-the-ordinary
she is a character — steeped in enigma – exotic and
flamboyant.
Jewish by birth
from the cradle up
ever loyal to the mysterious genealogy of roots
yet daughter in spirit to the Indigenous nations
she scatter her offerings of sacred tobacco
at the water's edge on Mimico Beach
we do this, she says, to honour the soul of native women

their strength and creativity, the weaving of their dreams
and the tragedy of their lost sisters.
She intones the words inspired by the eagle feather
to respect the land of the Mississaugas,
the Huron, Cree and Ojibway
her voice razor sharp in the frigid air
of a stark November morning
echoes across the vast canyon of watery expanse
gaining momentum with fervour of conviction,
swoop of a seagull, squawk of a goose
ends the ceremony with shamanic blessing.
It was Honey who caught the heartbreak
in the ancient Yiddish lament
immortalized by Verdi in "La Traviata"
and her re-creation in Spanish — Adios querido adios
pognantly exquisite has soothed the tears of many bereaved,
at the graveside of artist Norval Morrisseau
unfortunate martyr of an alien culture,
in funereal halls for Nahon Berhane
son of Eritrea murdered before his time,
sung again in remembrance of Leonard Cohen
and for the massacred women of Montreal.
Versatile as the changing faces at a masquerade ball
she is the same Honey
who gathers lilacs and graciously thanks the tree
who makes hummus and lavender cakes
serving those who might go hungry
and gently draws out the unique creativity
with affectionate warmth in a class of children,
as the Honey whose poetry lashes out
at the bullies, the unjust and the uncaring.
Never one to waste an opportunity
political activism always simmering just below the surface

female rights ever ready to spill out with the next breath
wherever there's an audience
she is a fire bursting its restraints
passionate in her plea for mercy for the wrongfully accused,
the homeless and the socially underprivileged.
Eloquent in prose, in poetry and in song
she challenges racial intolerance and abuse of women.
Beside her, I despise my passive non-chalance
pale as a green salad minus the green
like a dim-witted parrot repeating platitudes
before lapsing in mild amnesia,
yet she calls me her friend.
Honey – I salute her!
Saint and sinner all rolled in one
wearer of the laurels of a poet
the coxcomb of the jester
and the cabalistic veil of mystery.

Contents

POEMS FROM ME

The Blackness of AMazing

Blackness while prone comforts me.
Blackness while standing, personifies the fear
that if I am to go further into life
I must enter the blackness.

I imagine this non-colour as a swaddling cloth
wrapping me,
wrapping my fear,
my ignorance
until an edginess propels me
to reach for the light, any light
a light switch, a lighted path,
an enlightened idea.

Throughout this life's journey
I associate, mostly, with this amazing blackness -
the beatnik black of fashion,
diamond black hair dye,
Kohl black tracing the almond of my eyes,
the black macadam I traverse by car or on foot,
the blackness of being bad, sinful,
for wearing gothic black on lips that were punished
in a secondary school that didn't recognize
nor appreciate individuality,
experimentation or self-expression.

I could always rely on the amazing blackness
As I rely on night
turning day turning night again.

Pitch black always stumped me.
I could never fathom pitch black –
the sound of black -
not racial, but sound devoid of colour
and because I cannot see or hear this absence,
I celebrate possibility as it unfolds
against a backdrop of an AMazing blackness.

THE HIPPY DIPPY DREAM

Whatever happened to the hippy dippy dream?
The one that was about freedom -
free food, free love, free rent,
freedom from authority and clothes.
The dream itself revolutionized style, culture, ideas
in a beat heard round the world
picking up momentum
deafening to some
cloying, threatening those unaware, disinterested
the rhythm tolls the sound of the hippy dippy dream

Did the hippy dippy dream die
with the hippy dippy weatherman
glowing in the wind,
breathing hot, cold, technicolour
but dreaming, the tendril of smoke
mysteriously guiding the way
scattering dreamseeds, come what may?

Were you a dreamer of the hippy dippy dream?
Did you make love not war? Do you still?
Were you an herbal warrior smoking herb,
extolling its virtues while adding to the coffers
of big legal tobacco and chemical companies
while the dream, it would seem, became a gleam
in the eye of an accountants' ledgerbook?

Is the rainbow path of the hippy dippy dream
leading the queasy rider down a shaft of glut?

Has it metamorphosed
from flower power to the ivory tower
where dollars and urban scents
struggle to balance a tightrope scheme
that appeared to scuttle the hippy dippy dream?

Bury My Knee in My Wounded Heart

I will bury my knee in my wounded heart
and feel the taste of a whole year.
I will smell the lilacs and
get drenched in the rain and
hear the drum beating of my heart,
enjoining my voice in song.
Then my bony knee would rub the hurt
of my wounded heart and knead it gently,
gingerly, tenderly, as one kneads bread.
and like bread, this wounded heart
would be massaged, molded and sculpted into
becoming an offering.
This offering, given from the universe to my life,
would become the perfect gift,
the essential lesson, needed for my survival.

The Outrageous, Audacious Austin Tatious*

The is the story of Austin Tatious,
a salacious, mendacious, somewhat pugnacious man
who really loved bling.
BLING can be shiny or sparkly and dear
an outward display, a flawed character's veneer
BLING can be jewelry, embroidery or glitz
it doesn't matter, it's all 'puttin' on the ritz'.

His sense of delusion
resulted in the collusion
of Austin and some strangers who wanted bling.
The outrageous Austin Tatious
could be quite loquacious
especially when he wanted bling.

When he saw what he wanted,
some gaudy thing that could be flaunted,
he took it, despite anyone or anything.

Austin and cohorts went to market,
left the Hummer for the valet to park it
then went in search of some bling.
(Don't forget that...)BLING can be shiny or sparky and dear
an outward display, a flawed character's veneer
BLING can be jewelry, embroidery or glitz
it doesn't really matter because it's all ersatz.

They saw heirlooms and vacuums
some dust brooms and an old rattlesnake

BUT nothing would appease their slake.
They went for a stroll, feeling somewhat droll
yet, saw nothing they could take.
Soon tempers grew short,
between Austin and cohorts.
They just wanted to take and give naught in return.

Friendships are born without rancour or scorn
a sense of trust, goodwill, not feeling forlorn
but Austin Tatious wasn't perspicacious
and so he spent his life in search of BLING!

(Honourable Mention Award 2008 Stellar Literary Poetry Festival)

WHERE NATURE IS MY BEEHIVE

Where nature is my beehive,
there is freedom to flit, flee or frolic.
I could buzz as a honeybee,
fly at 20 mph using all 6 legs,
5 eyes and 2 sets of wings.
I could live in a colony, a sort of commune,
with workers, a Queen and drones.
As a female I could be Queen or worker.
Only males are drones and they do no work at all
since their job is to fertilize the Queen!
With 20,000 to 60,000 bees in a colony,
drones just drone.
It is no wonder that workers sting,
but only if feeling threatened.
Worker bees die once they sting.
Drones have no stinger.
Is this not an interesting look at male/female relations?
Queens have a stinger but they won't leave the hive
not even to help defend it.
I could be a Queen Honeybee
or a unionized labour bee sucking pollen
from flowers, blossoms or fields.
These days there is a mysterious honeybee holocaust.
Bees are dying by the thousands and no one knows why.
Not to scare my honeybee self,
maybe I could become another kind of creature spirit…
Where nature is my beehive
I fly, saunter, morph, exist on my terms.
Where nature is my beehive I am unfettered.

WELCOMING THE CRONE

What do you see when you look at me,
Your mother, gran'ma, sister, or auntie?
Well, that may be, but if that's all you see,
Let's talk a little philosophy.

CHORUS: The wrinkles are art,
I've got a big heart
I'm a crone, not prone to being invisible.

What do you see when you look at me
part of an Invisible Minority?
a statistic, simplistic, non-entity?
or, someone living with dignity?

I've got a voice, opinions, and that is power
The older I get, the less I cower.
speaking my mind is true liberation, I find
and I am welcoming the crone

CHORUS: The wattle is art,
It's parcel and part of,
a crone, not prone to being invisible.

I've got 3 chin hairs
and it's hard climbing stairs
but I'm here, you hear,
so, look at my personality.
or do you think age is a liability?

CHORUS: The crow's feet are art,
it's parcel and part, of a crone, not prone
to being invisible.

If I look invisible to you,
you must be blind,
cause you can't see,
a person trying to live with mutual respectability.
aging is a gift, a privilege that uplifts
and I AM welcoming the crone.

An Anecdote about Miss Ann Thrope and Ms. X. L. Ent

Miss Ann Thrope said to Ms. X. L. Ent,
"I have everything I need, I don't need to read!"
Well, X.L., taken quite aback,
began her compassionate attack…

"You might have everything you need, I see, but
you could never be all that you could be.
You could never gain greater perspective,
form an opinion, nor express a directive.
You could never make laws,
cure the heart of a jackdaw
nor ever have meaningful dialogue.
You could eat and shop and sleep and flirt,
you might even create a brand new shirt, but
to have a heart-to-heart with true value,
reading is the passport for this important avenue.
Think about it, and think very hard,
if you don't read and think and analyze,
you give your power to a wolf in sheep's disguise!"

Miss Ann Thorpe was duly shocked.
Her friend spoke to her honestly with words that truly rocked!!!
Miss Ann Thorpe thought long and hard
and then decided to try the Bard,
"To thine own self, be true," he said
and Ann wanted nothing more than a life sans rue.
So she studied every day,
phonetics, poems, narrative and essays.

She realized her true freedom lay in
readin' writin' and real communication.

She thanked X.L. profusely and gave her a huge hug,
for a friend in need is a friend in deed
and so they formed their very own creed.
> **"Read each day and write a bit,**
> **that way, you won't wind up a twit!!!"**

APPEARANCE MATTERS – Too White in a Room of Dark People, Too Dark in a Room of White People

I.   Appearance Is Important

The great contralto, Marian Anderson, was the first African-American to sing at the Metropolitan Opera in New York City. Our family rejoiced in her victory that day because her victory spoke to victory for all people of colour. My mother was a person of colour and was called "olive –skinned". I favour her colouring. Our muted, exalted celebration was an event that I'll never forget. It was also my 6th birthday.

II. Appearance Manifesting Everywhere Matters

There are many rivers flowing within me.
Placid and/or choppy blood memories,
(the Ganges, the Nile, the Dneipper, the Po, the Danube, the St. Lawrence)
like the currents, flavour behaviours of my living code
resulting in the intense diamond-like facet of my being.
Each facet makes up the imbroglio of me.
This imbroglio dictates how others see me.

III. Appearance Happens

It was Halloween in Toronto and my mother suggested I dress as a Gypsy to go trick or treating. It would cost her nothing as I would don her flowing skirt, peasant-style blouse with elasticized top worn off the shoulder, bright red lipstick, big looped earrings and a head scarf tied in the back.

When looking in the mirror, something happened. Dressing up no longer was about getting bags of candy, it was about identity. I couldn't put it into words then but that Gypsy image seemed to fit me. It gave me an authentic body memory sense of identity.

Being called a "gypsy" meant many things - the derivative of the word "Egyptian", a traveller, a romantic, passionate person or someone irresponsible.

IV. Appearances Matter

My maternal grandfather was North African (Moroccan, Ethiopian) piously Jewish, who married a Palestinian Desert pioneer from Austria. This grandfather had 3 wives and 9 children each, the story goes. Not one of any of the cousins got the North African colouring except me. My whole life was predicated on the fact that "I am different, the exception" like an excuse, a conclusion, a rationale!

Too white in a room of dark people and too dark in a room of white people and yes,

appearance matters.

V. Appearance as Lexicon

Appearances give license to vent opinions, judgements and bias.

Short of superficial cosmetic changes there's not a lot one can do about looks. As a young girl, I wasn't allowed to cut my hair. Hair became a language of pride with its lexicon of waviness, colouring, texture and length. Even though I've never bleached my hair, I dyed it auburn. When it was long I steam-ironed it straight, or wore statement-making Afro wigs and later Tina Turner spiked mane wigs.

There were times I worked on my body shape, believing that if I bound my breasts, wore 5 inch high heeled shoes, smeared on lighter or darker face paint, I could create a mask, a new conversation, a persona, a character, an illusion, an excuse to fit in. Nothing I did or would do, changed my skin colour, height, body shape or self esteem.

I really am too white in a room of dark people and too dark in a room of white people.

Never just this or that.

VI. Appearance Navigates

The euphemistic Yiddish word "NISHKA" means "Not this and not that". It defines a middle/mixed/meso swath navigating the Lifepath I would make.

VII. Appearances Matter Very Much

As a young vocalist working for the Mariposa Folk Festival, I was asked to work with the First Nations group. Many friendships grew out of that experience including a job offer with the Ontario Metis and Non-Status Indian Association singing in prisons for the Native Brotherhood and for the children. I heard that the Horseshoe Tavern was holding a press conference event to celebrate the cowboy. I borrowed that year's Ojibway Princess deer skin dress, braided my long hair into two plaits, wore a headband and feather and allowed my appearance to speak for a very pressing issue of the time, Wounded Knee. This "In-jew-n" attracted a lot of attention. At a time when it was important to bring that conversation to the forefront, I felt it was important to use theatre (humour, dress-up, timing, location) to express how much appearances make statements.

VIII. Appearances Are Important.

It matters very much that my reflection in the mirror is one I can identify with.

While others have called me "exotic', oriental, Spanish, shvartze (black) gypsy looking and other names, I do answer to a friendly voice.

Often this would serve to open doors for me, nurturing friendships, obfuscating things resulting in discomfort and confusion.

All my growing up life I didn't realize how different I looked because my mother bore the brunt of the criticism. She always smoothed over the racism saying defiantly, proudly "I am from "Ha'aretz" (the land, the Mediterranean, Middle East) When she was called olive-skinned, oriental, exotic, darkie, she silently screamed with her chin jutted out and a toss of her head "So what?" In time I would emulate this.

When asked, "Are you Burmese
                South Asian
                Aboriginal
        Spanish, Greek
        Indian
        Arab
        Oriental
        Jewish
        Italian, Portuguese, ...?

I would eventually learn to say "YES". Yes, I am. I am all of the above and more. I am whoever you want me to be.

IX. Appearances Matter

The reward of surviving name calling, ignorance and low self esteem, are lessons hard won. When travelling in Cuba, colour didn't seem as important as in North America. There are other places that recognize people as being people, human beings. There are many places but the trick is finding them. It must start with me. As Marion Anderson has famously said, "Everyone has a gift for something, even if that something is just being a good friend".

THE MOONSTONE AND LYSISTRATA

"…Oh, Moonstone, just when did he start going crazy?
And why? Imagine, when the lava pours
he wants me to be soundless
he wants a calm world yet is willing to wage a war
spawned only by his desires. Thoughtless.
I think he is insane. I love him, want him to be happy
even though he is madness personified.
he believes taking life – stoning, piercing, slaying
of another - is a means to an end, a solution. It. Is. Not.
I must stop this lunacy, Moonstone, this craziness.
My sister citizens must aid my plan.
I implore you, Moonstone,
give me strength. Rally my helpmates.
Help the clarity of my words reach their hearts
so that they will hear, then understand my intentions.
I want them to turn their backs defiantly disobeying
the men who want to use women's bodies.
My sisters must fulfill this audacity until such time
as all men, brothers, stop fighting each other.
For when the fire starts first in the inner thigh,
it burns, until consumed by the blood of the legs,
loins, belly, entire being.
Sisters of Solidarity, we must not be tempted
by the allure of this heat. We must become like you,
Moonstone: immovable.
Just as musicians look at the shapely lyre
and want to play it, men look at women's forms
and want to play us as their instruments.

Moonstone, help me rail my sisters so that they will not
flter in withholding their charms from their men
they must understand that by going on a conjugal strike
they, too, are fighting the battles of war. Thus,
my sisters and I become warriors in the name of peace!!!"

COMME LES YEUX PETILLANT

Sparkling determination,
Like bright eyes
Illuminated my resolve.

Life Is Beautiful When

life is beautiful when
things flow in rhythm,
when there is trust between strangers
and fear is melted by the look of another's eyes.

there's beauty that sings and beauty that gives
rise to dreams that have never been realized

life is the continuum that connects
the point of birth and the departure of death

life is beautiful when
I wake up in the morning and feel
the need to greet the sun,
the noise of traffic,
the song of the raven-coloured crow and the speckled thrush.
The song of my heart rumbles from sleep,
growls from hunger,
yearns to express love and
recognizes the inter-connectedness of all that lives

life is beautiful when
I feel I can do
something for someone else as well as something for myself

life is beautiful when
I pay homage to that which
I can't see and to that which I can

New Reality

I'm driving in to the colours of autumn
Trying to escape life's drudgery
Realizing turning off the t.v.
Is too easy because shying away from suffering
Is like thinking it won't affect me.

We are living in a new reality
The world changed from what it used to be
That's like you and me
Recognizing we are awakening from our reverie.

The mystical phoenix rises
Leading a flame strewn trail
Separating goodness and evil
While discerning opinions on the exhale.

It is the kindness of strangers
Who help without being asked
To build bridges of friendship
Creating value that will last

It is all about perspective
Do you take sides , which one are you on?
What if you are walking the middle way
Encompassing all sides, that is not a conundrum

There is no right or no wrong
Only goodness or banality
We must create a perspective
To guide us through this new reality.

TOFU STEW RAP **

Tofu Stew is what I'm making with you,
And this is what we're going to do.
Heat the pan with a little bit of oil,
Not too much or it's going to broil.
Cut up garlic and onion small
Saute them until they enthral.
Add carrots, tomatoes, et al
But add them later when we've done it all.

Pour some water and bouillon in the pan
Watch as it browns and wait till it boils.
Cut tofu into small chunks
Then boil it up like meatless hunks.

Add some parsnips cause they taste real sweet.
Yukon Gold potatoes are such a treat.
Include noodles of bean vermicelli
They look like glass and fill up your belly.

When everything you want is in the pan,
Cook a while, smile a while
Spice it up or rice it up.
Smell the flavour and taste its savour
Taste till you crave
All that goes into
Tofu Stew.

** published in "The Literary Gourmet" and "Fireweed"

WALTZ OF JOY

(Should be spoken or sung in waltztime – make up melody as you
go along)

Come dance with me a dance of joy
A dance of joy forever
Like friends who love each other.

I wish to be dancing forever
Believing it might just happen
Wishing enough times, makes things happen.
Recognizing even if I'm sad, I can be happy.

Standing, not dancing is too easy
But that can be hard to accept.
So, let's dance like a waltz through the pages of time,
Like friends evolving from strangers.

Let's dance the same dance but in a new light
Like time's musings in a mirror.

Let's waltz for the beauty that is seen in that mirror
For beauty is where you find it.

Look as we dance
For what we see is what will be
Like a suntan's glow being tended.

Let's dance into time, palm in palm entwined
Joy knows the days have come
Joy knows that time held in the palm of your hand,
Is today creating tomorrow

WAR AIN'T NOTHIN' BUT THE BLUES

War ain't nothin' but the blues
Guaranteed to make everybody lose
Using righteous indignation as an excuse
To justify each horrific act of abuse.

War ain't nothin' but an excuse
That lets misunderstanding play fast and loose
While ignorance rules the roost
Saying, 'UGLY or UGLIER is the road to choose'.

War ain't nothin' but the blues
Each song and story is more bad news.
WAKE UP NOW!!! 'cause if you snooze, you lose –
Sleepwalking in life is no luxury cruise.

War ain't nothin' but the blues
Survival is only one of the avenues
That force people to seek life's truths
Using animal instincts to amuse or confuse.

War ain't nothin' but the blues,
Dreams evaporate - leaving dingy, blurred hues
Of hopeful memories guarding secret clues.
War, like peace, lives in our hearts enthused,
Challenging, "Which one do you choose?'

DON'T GET SAD, GET MAD

Chorus:
Don't get sad, get mad
Get going, DO Something (about it)!

Are you blind to the circumstances of the world?
Do you live your life, like an ostrich with your tail to the sun?
If you do, this song isn't for you, so

Chorus:
Don't get sad, get mad
Get going, DO Something (about it)
But don't hurt anybody, not even a tad when you're mad
Cause that won't help anybody

Do you let other people tell you what to do –
Falling in line, monkey see, monkey do?
If you do, this song isn't for you, so….

Chorus:

Do you speak up loud when there's something to say?
Is your upper lip stiff while you bite your tongue?
If you do, this song isn't for you, so…

Chorus:
Don't get sad, get mad
Get going, Do Something (about it), like write a poem,
Or sing a song, call someone close
And give them a dose of what's on your mind,

Ask for help, and pray for courage,
Do a dance, shake your fist, and give someone just the gist of
What's on your mind,
Make up your own things to do that would be the best for you.

Brilliant. Even Now. (for Ron)

Brilliant.
A word usually reserved for stars or sunlight
Is how I feel about you. Even now.

Electrified intensity.
A powerful motion
Happened when I first met you.

A serene thought of spiritual inspiration
Propels me to write about you.

My open hand offered
In curiosity and with a sense of adventure.
You grasped it and drew it to your breast.
Like the alchemist's gold, my heart, my spirit
Melded into your heart and your spirit.

Climactic scenes of an everyday opera
Played out life's lessons loudly, privately, publicly, intimately
Entwining like English ivy until we grew separate.

Warm affection and eternal appreciation
Courses through my blood
Transcending the earthiness of my being
And remembers the love for you
That will live in my heart forever.

Peace, The Attainable Goal

Peace is a river
that flows incessantly,
eternally, through everyday life.

It isn't judgmental
or even definable, it just
is.

It kisses both lovers and
warriors, embracing both.

Peace is a goddess, an alchemist, a magician,
a great hope, eternal lamp of guiding warmth.
It is an ideal that causes misunderstandings.
It is an unlit, secret candle in a darkened cave.
Peace lives in the hearts of those who desire tomorrow.

Peace is a purpose for living – the great
Attainable inheritance
That which is bestowed and willed to all who
Seek the truth of existence,
The dependent origination of interconnectedness.

Peace is a song without ending and a
reason to wake up each morning refreshed and ready
to greet the challenges and gifts of each day.

Peace is more than a yearning for no more war.
Peace is more than recognition of the serene heart.

Peace is you and me and ignorance and suffering and
embracing that then transforming it into a goal of cooperation.

Peace walks with all who have open eyes and a caring heart.
Peace sings the songs that need to be heard by all those
willing to listen.

Peace exists amid turmoil, challenge, regret, disappointment.
It is the magic carpet that transports a heart daring
to go to new horizons and greater depths.

YOU CAN TAKE THE GIRL OUT OF THE NEIGHBOURHOOD

You can take the girl out of the neighbourhood
 But you can't take the neighbourhood out of the girl
OH No   (That's right)
Because the neighbourhood is a good
Place to learn and grow and become   (That's right)

Just like seeds sprout and blossom   (That's right)
Just like babies walk and talk   (That's right)
Just like neighbours care and share   (That's right)

So you can take the boy out of the neighbourhood
 But you can't take the neighbourhood out of the boy
OH No   (That's right)
Because the neighbourhood is a good
Place to bring people together   (That's right)

It's a healthy place   (That's right)
And a beautiful space   (That's right)
And people have grace   (That's right)

So you can take people out of the neighbourhood
But you can't take the neighbourhood out of ME (THAT''S RIGHT)

You can take me out of the neighbourhood
But you can't take the neighbourhood out of me
OH NO, cause the "hood" is good
no could, no should, let's not be misunderstood
cause the neighbourhood is good   (THATS RIGHT!!!)

Those Eyes

As you lay curled up on a pillow at her feet
it is those eyes that tell the story
they have to
the face is veiled, masked, humbled
temptation may befall the viewer
she is beautiful and knows how to string you along
one thread of a story, at a time
you see her everywhere
you have to, it is Covid-19 and all must be masked
you have no choice but to trust her eyes
you can't see her smile
you don't know if she is a brilliant actor
all you know is that she looks at you
that's all you get

she might be Salome, named for peace in Hebrew
associated with duplicity
she lives today in the eyes above the masked veil
where she dances to the tune of a synthesizer
and leaves you wanting more
you long for more
we all long for more
more smiles and more eye contact
we beseech the stars and the moon
we bay and howl and learn to survive
we see our breath in the air
but only if we take off our masks on a cold night
if we dare
maybe she is Scheherezade, narrator, storyteller of

histories in the making
giving each curlicue of a snippet all the more reason
to want to be near her

Is she beautiful? We don't know.
We only think we care.
Will the ending be happy?
Will she teach us to hitchhike
on a comet floating through the nightskies of the unknowable?
How do we maintain our humanity?
That's the question you really want answered.
You have expectations of her
she doesn't care about expectations
she cares about connections

She says, "in acting as a human being
my starlight shines as well as yours in the dark sky.
Trust, know that we both shine, know
the night sky is more dazzling with many stars shining".

she gives you what you want
she gives you the illusion of effervescent dreams
she gives you hope
you must take it and swallow it
you must take off your mask
you must dare
you must feel all that is written on your face
before you are compelled to don your mask
it is mandated
once more to be stalwart, patient, caring
It is you who must stand
for all that is attainable
as you lay curled up on a pillow at her feet

A Frayed Knot

I am afraid, not
I am a frayed knot
unravelling, revealing
vulnerabilities once hidden
now shared with almost no one

threads entwined, braided, knitted
transforming communities of singing life choirs
they now mesh with the enticing winds and roaring tides

this is a-lone-ness language, needing to be heard
relearned ex-harmony, ex-vocabilities, redefined

"Adapt or Die" is the new motto
"Adapt and Live" is the new mantra
INNOVATE, regurgitate, realign, be grateful

Once in a land far away the chickadee and nuthatch
fought for territory,
once in a land faraway I dared hug you
now in this land inhabited by an invisible death scourge
I keep my distance, I keep my counsel
I remember my dreams

I am a frayed knot
looking to once again bind
all that I love

Patience, they tell me is the key
the Key of Patience
the knot dangling from a new music

EVERYTHING IS RELATED – A Philosophy of the Voice and Healing

Everything is related, or interconnected.
If not for air, we could not breathe.
Water keeps us alive longer than food.
The body is mostly water.
Part of the job of being a serious singer, recognizes
the body as a vocal instrument. Understanding
the connection of the voice to breath, water, sound vibration,
self-expression, diet, intellectual or artistic awareness,
physical experience as well as issues of esteem.

We need their torso to sing but not their arms and legs.
Croaking out one or two notes is all the sound some people can
muster.
If that is all the sound one evokes, in sincerity, that is a form of
beauty.
A hearing impaired person who is not totally deaf,
expresses themselves with one or two notes.
No one needs to sound like Pavarotti to communicate beauty.
If you can speak, you can sing.

Music or the language of sound is also interconnected.
One note by itself is one note.
One note in relation to another is a musical relationship and has a
name, "interval".
That interval is connected to the perception of the ear.
How the ear hears that note is another relationship – that of the
listener.
The listener forms a relationship with the sound that

evokes a memory, a feeling, or an idea.
That relationship can then be expressed to an audience,
even if that audience is just the wall, it still is important and
is the relationship between performer, or creator and audience.
All is interconnected.

When one recognizes the beauty of sound,
The PROCESS of creation must be developed.
It is integral to the healing process.
Healing is related to the word WHOLE.
So an idea, begat in the heart or mind of a creative person
willing to explore that creativity will eventually express something
of a greater wholeness.

In time, with a deeper intention to manifest sound, discipline is
learned.
Sometimes creativity is natural.
It is intuitive and comes without thinking.
Part of the creative process is recognizing the intuitive aspect.
Intuition, I believe, is a natural part of the human being.
When intuition is not recognized or acknowledged,
the chance of the human being becoming out of balance,
out of sync or out of sorts becomes greater
And the chances of illness are greater.

When people recognize the integration of and simultaneity of
physical experiences harmonizing with energy of the spirit,
intentionally offering awareness of the mind,
a whole experience is the result.
This is a truth of the performance stage as well as for those
recovering from any illness or trauma.
This is braiding the body, mind and spirit.
This braid includes hope, light, and inspiration
and a profound sense of interconnection.

Shoes Blues (to be spoken, if possible, read aloud, rhythmically)

When you've got the clues that your shoes are giving you the blues and you need some good news on the views you gotta take, it might be time to lose those blues when you choose to buy some new shoes

Buy shoes at the end of the day, your feet swell cause they're swell but they've worked hard all day and they are a different size than they were in the morn (don't mourn) it's just a fact of life

When we get older, our feet get bolder and change the way the bones lay and change the way the muscles play and change the size that they've been all day. Some gain weight, others lose the poundage, ounces, kilos, grams whatever, which has an effect on your shoe size. One foot is larger than the other, don'tcha know and that is something we all should know

Before you buy shoes, try them on, walk a little and stand a lot and that should help to know if they are a perfect fit , or not

Always leave a little room between your big toe and the shoes' big toe, maybe a centimetre is the way to go, the clue you need when you're buying a shoe for speed

Don't buy shoes thinking "I'll break them in", they're not a horse of course and you'll never win. If you want them to stretch, don't forget, do yoga

Fungi, not mushrooms, bloom in the room in the soles of your shoes, if you can don't wear the same shoes two days in a row, buy an extra pair and rotate them before you go, shopping, running, walking, whatever the weather, now and forever

And then there's the plagues:

Ingrown toenails, bunions, Hammertoes, neuromas, fallen arches, plantar fasciitis, plantar warts, pump bump, Achilles tendonitis. Some are genetic, some come from shoes, giving your feet the blues but all of them treatable, like cut toe nails straight across, orthotics, insoles, surgery, arch supports, over the counter lotions and potions

There's one thing that I know, and I'll tell you before I go, and that is our feet, our soul's soles take the brunt of our weight and our soul's soles must be honoured whether you're an athlete, a dancer, a singer or just you.

When we take care of our feet, we stand up tall, balanced, secure and confident.

What we care for, cares for us and that includes our feet!!!

THE SECRET INGREDIENT

My mother was one of 27 children. My grandfather, a dark-skinned, Jewish Moroccan/Ethiopian/Egyptian/(Falasha) Halutz (pioneer) settled in Palestine in the late 1800s.

He sired 9 children, each, with 3 wives, the last one of whom, my grandmother, emigrated to Palestine from Austria. I think of myself as a Continental Mix, a mongrel.

I've met 3 of my mother's brothers, uncles from Paris, England and Canada and 2 of my mother's sisters, aunts who lived in Israel and California. They are all from the last brood of the 27 or 9, whichever way one looks at it. My mother was number 25 or 7. She, herself, had 7 pregnancies. I am number 7, the 7th child of the 7th child. All of my mother's siblings were born in Palestine/Israel, or as they call it "Ha'aretz, The Land". All the siblings physically and facially resemble one another. All scattered to varying points of the Diaspora.

During World War I (WWI), when Palestine was under the British Mandate, Uncle Chaim, who emigrated to England, joined the British Armed Forces. He kept a photo of Auntie Leah in his pocket. One time, in the military, Chaim showed Leah's photo with her long, wavy, uncut hair cascading over her Rubenesque torso, to a fellow soldier, a Canadian, also Jewish. On sight, Sam the Upholsterer, asked Uncle Chaim if he could marry Auntie Leah and bring her to Canada. As all the siblings were orphaned due to consumption (tuberculosis), the elder children looked after the younger ones and Chaim married off his sister sight unseen (or so the rumour went). But Leah wanted out of the desert, far from the land of the hot sun, sand dunes, fig trees, date and Royal Palms where water had to be hand pulled from wells in buckets (where once the child, Uncle Pesach/Percy fell nearly to his death and had to be rescued). Leah wanted to be far from the burning sun but didn't expect to come to a land of ice or humidity, snow, many kinds of fierce storms including the immigrants' harsh reality.

Auntie Leah was a gifted Tarot card fortune-teller. She set up shop at the kitchen table on the upper floor of a 2 family residence in downtown Toronto near Bathurst and Dundas Streets. This was a Jewish enclave of immigrants, mainly from Europe. Leah was darker skinned and exotic in this mix of factory workers. This was part of the tapestry known as the Garment District. In the early 1920's, after WWI, The Roaring Twenties or the Jazz Age to some, a haven for many, hopes and dreams were all that kept many people surviving. Many of these citizens of Toronto wanted to bring family members to Canada for a "better" life where the rumour was, "the streets were paved in gold" and Communism was just beginning to bubble in the hearts of some, but not in this story, except that Emma Goldman lived in the neighbouring vicinity.

Many people came to consult Auntie Leah who read them their destinies in the arcanas of the Tarot. Auntie Leah made enough money to pay for passage for my mother and then my Uncle Percy and Auntie Esther. Esther, a teenager at that time, was making her way west and stopped in Marseille, France where she caught the eye of a man who would become her husband, and then partner in the Hagganah, a clandestine part of the Jewish military, fighting for independence from the British, in order to build the Jewish State of Israel. This was how they built and then lived out their lives, dedicated to themselves, their family and their cause.

In time, my mother met my father at the Canada/Palestine Club. She valued his intelligence, strength, love of Shakespeare, science and opera, and his politics. She called him handsome. They were Zionists, idealists. He also partnered with her in finances – he would work and every Friday hand over the paycheck. She dealt with the household expenses. My father was given an allowance, keeping some spending money for himself but she was the chief operating officer. My mother claimed that was what kept their marriage together, that trust and partnership. He just adored her, plain and simple – her beauty, her cooking, her social skills and sensitivity. He also accepted her family as his. My father's mother and sibling remained in Palestine where they would die of consumption. His father left for America and wound up in Chicago where kind family members included my grandfather into their family get-togethers. My grandfather was a vegetarian in the same historical movement that inspired George Bernard Shaw to vegetarianism – harm no one. Because the United States wasn't under the British Mandate, Yiddish, not Hebrew, was the primary language, pastrami or brisket, not hummus, the food of choice. Hummus, the middle eastern mash of chick peas, sesame butter, lemon and olive oil would become prevalent and much eaten in the future but at this time it was unknown. The Middle-Easterners learned the Eastern European cuisine of borscht, dill pickles and the smoked meat deli. This was the new cultural norm.

One food thing seemed to be constant - grated potato patties or pancakes or latkes. It is said that the difference between great latkes and just delicious latkes is the love found in the tiny drop of blood occurring when the person, usually a woman, the balabosta (female head of the house), grated the potato and didn't notice her fingers getting too close to the sharp grater. Thus, the love for her family, dripped ever so tiny into the grated potatos, made all the difference in flavour. At least that's what my mother told me but she said it was THE SECRET INGREDIENT. (If anyone sees my knuckles bandaged or scraped, don't ask).

The melding of cultures occured in the kitchen. Because yogurt was a Middle Eastern staple and not sour cream, sometimes one was substituted for the other. Soup was made with yogurt or sour cream, or used as a side dish, a "for-shpiet". At the kitchen table or counter, committees were formed, businesses started, families entwined, old angers and unrequited histories were left in the sand dunes of time.

It took time for everyone to settle into a new life, a new culture, a new climate, a new hope. In time and in this melange, I came after WWII. I didn't ever meet my grandparents, not even the Chicago grandfather, Gershon, a Hebrew name that can be translated as something akin to "stranger in a strange land" in its Yiddish meaning, a "stranger in exile' or sojourner. He died when I was seven.

There were harbingers of old damages, invisibly swirling in our domicile - unkissed hurts and untended bureaucracies. My father claimed his father didn't fill in proper papers for him to live in the U.S.A. Fortunately, I believe, because he had a Passport from Palestine, he could come and live in Canada, another one of Britain's colonies, meet my mother and create me. Regrettably, he missed his Chicago family and their culturally enriching lifestyle – kindness, tolerance, books, music, discussion, hopes and ambitions. I understood him completely. My mother's family, the Palestinian Canadians worked hard, gambled, didn't follow intellectual pursuits, were into fashion and read tabloid magazines. Still, it was Gershon who was named the stranger in exile and not my father. Nevertheless, my father joined the Royal Institute for Science and went to lectures in science and astronomy. My father enjoyed Charlie Chaplin, Marx Brothers films and read Shakespeare all the while delivering milk with a horse and wagon. He was the last person in the City of Toronto to deliver milk with a horse and wagon. As he would remind me, I was able to attend the Royal Conservatory of Music, from that delivery service, (well, that and the Baby Bonus cheques, courtesy of the Canadian government).

And still we ate and prospered with the providence of time. The State of Israel was born 6 months before me. My parents bought a house and welcomed survivors of the Holocaust, as well as Jewish survivors of the McCarthy Era persecution and even, ironically, Christian Evangelical missionaries who tried to convert us.

As my mother used to say, "we've never been poor because we always had food on the table".

Beets grated and boiled with water and a shank bone made a scrumptious borscht soup. You were allowed to slurp it until it dripped down the chin onto the napkin. That was a real sign of the good life.

In 1960, when I was 11 years old, my mother'n'father (one word, not a mistake) decided they could afford to send my mother and me back to Israel to re-meet her sister. 36 years had passed since they'd seen each other. All they had were letters to keep in touch. It was our first plane ride. To me everything was exciting but my mother's ankles swelled on the plane. We stopped in Rome and Paris and finally landed in the State of Israel. At that time, we had to disembark by ladder. Many people reached the ground, bent and kissed the earth. Then we were "accosted" by lepers. This was my welcome to Israel. From Elvis via El Al to Eilat. Finally we came to Auntie Esther's home where part of the land was rented to a movie company making a film called "Exodus". In time, I would have the privilege of meeting Oscar-nominated actor Sal Mineo but that's a story for another day and time. My mother broke her arm at the beginning of our trip and stayed home. I learned to cull cactus fruit, hang out with kids who didn't speak English as I couldn't speak Hebrew. I missed my father, my liberal, progressive, beloved father as I was now 11 and looked 15 under the roof of a man who didn't have daughters. I had never been objectified before. I had never gone back in time. All that I learned, including having a gun pointed at me when I unknowingly wandered into "No Man's Land" would serve me, would shape how I view the world. In the meantime, my mother was dealing with what war, sickness and poverty foist upon all people, regardless of where they come from and what they look like.

For all the years my parents supported the creation of the State of Israel, she was invited to a state dinner by Prime Minister Ben Gurion. Too bad they didn't invite the kid. Oh well... My mother relearned to make hummus. My mother began a journey of reclaiming her heritage, dark skin, curly hair and self-pride. In the meantime, my father ate every day at a restaurant called "The Bagel". He survived. This 3 months apart changed everyone. In retrospect, I think, the 3 months apart and cultural reacquaintanceship was all for the better. At the time, we were all re-learning who we were.

I came back to discover the 1960s. Music, fashion, puberty. My parents weren't quite ready. Just wait, Bob Dylan was on the horizon as were the hippies. Fortunately, in Israel, they smoked the "nargilla" Peace pipe (lol) and so that aspect of the culture was a little familiar. They understood kibbutz living and so communal living was also understood. Hindsight is the greatest gift.

With "the secret ingredient" as previously mentioned earlier in this narrative, comes DNA. I believe, it is through this life thread that I inherited a culture, a lore, a behaviour and a sense of identity. I feel the sentient ties of taste and smell and image. I offer this sensory experience to others and thus connect not just to my family history but to a new family creation. As we say at the dinner table, "Enjoy"!!!

Anywhere But Here

"You've got to leave the table when love's no longer being served."
Nina Simone

And there it was, beautiful with crystal goblets,
whiter than snow linen tablecloths and napkins,
the brightest burgundy on an opulent table
yet it was all so empty
devoid of laughter and warmth
and so I left
to where?
Well, even the word "anywhere" has **"here"** in it
going away yet remaining still
becoming like the emperor moth gestating for years
emerging from an egg to an adult,
until finally at the last stage
the caterpillar spins a cocoon, dissolving completely
liquidizing, morphing into something
completely different – an emperor moth.
Resistance is what it fights on its way out of the cocoon.
Fighting resistance is never easy.
Not every fight to be reborn is a victory.
Some don't make it.
I am not the emperor moth, but I learn
from its struggles where no better place
than here is where I take my first step
of a journey to my own resilience

Bomb Sniffing Plants

(based on research by Dr. June Medford, Colorado State U.)

This is extraordinary, albeit very true.
Do you know bomb sniffing plants are being developed to protect you.
By 2014, in every major airport, they're designed especially to
protect you.

Full body scanners and pat downs intrude
so plants with special sensors deigned not to be rude
will turn white, signalling a bomb is in "the hood".

The lead researcher tells us that plants can't run or hide,
they have a special detecting language used to describe
threats from bombs. When vegetation turns white, that is the guide.

This is how it works — receptors designed on computers
transfer into vegetation, rewires the plant.
The receptors take information outside the plant
to information inside said plant
When specific bomb information is detected, a circuit is turned on
and tells the plant "TURN WHITE", (that turns me on).

The technology is transferable into any plant.
Exquisite orchid, serene hosta, any floral resident
can then sniff out a bomb-wielding, petulant mendicant.

Plants are 10 times more effective than any sniffing dog
yet here's one bit of information that is just a cog -
they can't detect people - ONLY explosives, are you all agog?

The times they are a-changing, surveillance is apace
sensory development is the name of the new race
and all sentient beings are the cadre in this brand new place.

Eye to the Sky. Twist.

the apple orchard farmer directed our group of pickers
to hold the apple in our palm,
(the apple bottom is the eye)
eye to the sky, twist
that's how the apple comes off the branch
eye to the sky, twist
don't yank, just let it press into the palm of your hand
the tree lets it go

somehow that's how I see letting go
looking skywards, trusting the blue
or the puffy, sometimes wispy clouds

I don't always want to let go
I feel the connections to others
I feel the part of you that is me
I look for me in you
and when I don't see you,
I hear a silence louder than a roar

a saffron October misty morning
before a season of impending winter,
walking, I think
the summer had gone swiftly,
autumn didn't last very long
or did it?
did I miss autumn while coping
with the murder of an associate
or death by cancer of two others?

yet, I am very grateful that two dear friends
are still here hanging on and hanging in
surviving heart attacks and fear

I asked the orchard farmer
how can I pick apples from the tree
as I am so short?
he said, "walk into the tree, the lower branches
of the trees are fruitful
don't touch the bud
grab the apple, mould your grasp to it
turn the eye, the bottom of the apple, skywards
twist
the apple will come into your hand
they are ready to let go of their branch life
and become food for you."

I can't help but think of Eve offering Adam an apple
they call it the fruit of knowledge
of the tree of death and life
the forbidden fruit -
I call it an amazing experience
pick apple, brush apple
aim apple towards lips
mould teeth to an apple spot
and bite
the juice will run down your chin
your taste buds will love it
your jaws will chew and chew and masticate
and the fibre will be absorbed by your digestion
it's a luscious experience, primordial
primitive

It is the time of a new year, harvest-time
time to cut apple slices and
drizzle honey on them, it is a celebration
once the bees were going into oblivion
but now many are back giving us the fluid of their labour
we could not let go of them
they gave us the celebratory honey,
this viscosity of sweetness
and with the apple we are reminded
yesterday was then,
let go of the night
golden light comes a-dawning
until it is time to let that go
darkness, like a veil, offers the mystique of decision
it, too, is a gift
until it is time to let that go
and like picking the apple from the limb
eye to the sky, twist

Give Me a Nickel

Give me a nickel
I'll tell you again
the male is a rooster
the female, a hen
don't ask me when
don't ask me how
don't ask me why
they named a clock "Big Ben"

Give me an apple
and I'll tell you again
lions sleep in a lair, bears hibernate in a den
girls become women and boys become men
a plume is a feather and dipped in ink
becomes a pen

a pen is mightier than a sword
my honour lies in giving you my word
I tell no lies and I spin no yarn
the cat loves sunning itself in the barn

the seasons are changing
time waits for no one
each morning I wake is
a miracle unsung

My Diaphanous Love Manifesto

I am a hot house tomato basking in the sun
temperature controlled, happy, full of fun.
How can I describe what love means to me,
why should you believe what my eyes see?
LOVE, 4 letters, is such a big word
mistaking romance and excitement for love can be absurd.

If love means being your cheerleader and champion, too -
I ask only the same of you.

If you are my reflection then I am your gift
one rewards the other without any short shrift.

There are times to question and people to doubt
time in solitude discovers this noble route.

I see my love manifest everywhere
challenging fear, poison and despair.
It's up in the trees and down by the lake
free as a bird and low as a snake.

I wish for you what I want for me
good health, joy and endless possibility.

Good friends try to make each other happy
caring, doing or being 'sappy',
love is a gift, receive its due
things given in love are meant for you.
Intentions wholesome and utterly pure

hears your heart beating, of that you can be sure.
I am imperfect, sincere, a cyclone and a deer,
a gentle blossom ready to appear
mostly scared, a little scarred,
sometimes a little unprepared.

There are times I take more than I give
there's a lot to value in the life I live.
Other times I give, expecting nothing in return -
either way they're lessons, things I've got to learn.

Take these words from a hot house tomato -
love, when guilelessly given returns tenfold
happiness may manifest sooner than later
unexpectedly appearing, like a miracle to behold.

The Language of Colours

I am the prism of my being
I attract the sun, breaking each sunbeam
    into a glorious rainbow
each hue has a message —
feel us with your heart not with your eyes
know that the blue of water changes
    from icy white to dark, threatening blue
    to serene turquoise or hopeful green
know that true diamonds sparkle off each wavelet
know that the bright orange of the Sunday
    is a mix of red and yellow —
very few things are purely tinted
know that blue and yellow become the green of grass
taste her – you might like her taste or
use her as you would blow a whistle
know the brown of the earth can be black or red —
    it depends where you stand

all the colours of the spectrum guide you
they live invisibly and visibly
they live in our sense of touch, taste and smell
yes, colours can be formed, tasted, felt or textured
know that black is labeled devoid of colour
that is not true
black comforts, black shines
black carries all colours just as white does
there is no purity of colours
on each shoulder is a rainbow
it becomes wings

it becomes a magic flying carpet
it wraps you in elegance
and comforts you in lush abundance
it will speak to you
learn the language of colours

I Am A Zing

I am a zing
I AM a zing
I am A zing
I am a ZING
I, amazing

zings are the light you see emanating from the centre of the sun

zings are the shadows appearing at the end of the day
they were there all along but they only showed up
when the sun went behind the horizon

zings are what you get when you pray for clarity
like looking in a microscope or opera glasses
adjusting them and then – zing, it's all clear
like hope after despairing pleas

zings are invisible messages winds bear
in waves and circles and breezes
they blow hot, cold, strong or gentle

I am a zing
I AM a zing
I am A zing
I am a ZING
I, amazing

A Speck of Time

There on the horizon
can you see it? That speck
between the cloudless blue of the sky
and the white-capped wavelets of the sea?
Oh, it's not a speck, it's a boat.
I guess it all depends on one's perspective,
distance, vantage point.
The closer I come, the more the object changes
like someone's opinion.

But that speck (boat) is bobbing
and people on it are sunning and rocking.
In my Gulliver's Lilliputian fantasy,
the longer I stare at this speck,
the longer my plasticine imagination
determines how that speck changes
or if it stays the same.

There are times I can hold that speck in the palm
of my musings, create a scenario and then
just let it go.
There are other times it is like rubbing a Genie's lamp
expecting the mirage to carry me away.
It is a wonderful, peaceful way to spend a moment,
in a speck of time.

Writing the Silence

Silence.

Silence is revealed to writers, painters, singers and other artistic disciplines through listening. How? Some people think silence is devoid of sound. It is not. Birds' wings beating in flight make a rhythmic melodys. We cannot hear it. Yet, if we came cose enough, the rhythm would enrance us. There are many melodies that are unheard but they exist. Sonar, underwater songs go fast or slow.

Again I ask, how dow we write the silent language of the living universe? Perhaps with a certain discipline we can begin to tune into this language.

Sit in a chair with feet flat on the floor,

let the coccyx, the bottom bone of the spine, the lower back touch the chair.

Make sure the spine is straight.

Just listen for a minimum of 30 seconds.

This is not a meditation.

This is active listening.

It is the basis of all art forms.

It is how Beethoven was able to compose while being deaf.

It is how some people think themselves into concentration.

Writing is not lonely when it is thought of as an action, an act of doing.

Yes, we are alone when writing but it is a form of focusing on listening to the depths of our own self-expression that we want to bring forth and share.

Active listening tunes our ears to focus on silence or sound.

Become aware of all that you "observe" with your ears. Do you live on a busy street with lots of traffic? Does the flow of traffic sound like a symphony, getting louder or softer? When the phone rings does your ear flinch or can you tell what note it is? What sounds do you hear in your daily life?

Does the opening and closing of a drawer draw your attention? The sound of running water in the sink or shower? How does listening to people who speak other languages capture your attention?

Often we describe "soundless observations" as "nothing". Something devoid of sound is not nothing. When we train our ears to hear beyond our expectations, we open to a whole new world of wonder.

Some people in big cities are aware of the cadences of traffic.

In the country it could be the clatter of birdsong.

In stillness it could be the pulsation of blood flowing through the veins.

Active listening is a true exercise.

A Camp Called the Sublime*

From the profound depths of isolation
I turn the door knob leading out
to the unoccupied hallway of the unknown

My destination is to the sublime land of the
roosting swan

The hallway carpet patterns are like dizzying waves
to traverse these I need the cool confidence of
a deep sea surfer championing the high waves
onto the exit door leading down
stony concrete stairs to the garage
where my expectant car awaits

Extending the side mirror, opening the door
I drop my bag and mold my body
into the driver's seat contours and away we go

Yes, there is a gingko tree enroute on this, our home
on native land. It is beautiful and health-giving
like many immigrants -
all living near pine, cedar, tamarack and maple
diversity is the new buzzword

Onwards we go, me and my trusty red chariot
southbound to the shore

My apartment, my camp of the sublime womb is
warm, comforting and devoid of humans -
the tv informs me, the phone connects me

the computer beckons me to interact -
nothing replaces human contact

Once I had a dream of singing with the Exquisite Prince Mood
of the Disordered Clan
I no longer seek this fantasy
it disturbs my sense of myself
now I seek omens from the invisible "shoten zenjin" -
(the universal protective forces) -
no traffic accidents, no arguments
nothing lost
that is the message I bank on

Crossing grids of pedestrian traffic, car traffic, bikes and strollers
onwards to the highway where once stood
Sunnyside Amusment Park
I have never forgotten the merry-go-round
jumping on a moving circle was exhilarating

Finally, I arrive at the camp of the sublime roost of swans
who waits for me to appear, I believe

gulls always circle over waters still or roiling
sometimes geese and ducks stake claim to their territory
but if I'm lucky, it is the swans, those other immigrants
the ones whose neck form heart to heart love stories
that bring to life the magical, mystical serenity
with a message that says
"be serene, learn resilience, show yourself in beauty
and swim, paddle,
forever value the camp of the sublime"

"a camp called the sublime" is a line from Liz Howard's poem
"Psychogeometry" in her book "Infinite Citizen of the Shaking Tent"

WHAT DOES MY FRIENDSHIP MEAN TO YOU?

"...you've got to learn to leave the table when love's no longer being served..."
                                        Nina Simone

WHAT does my friendship mean to you?

When meeting me,
There are some people,
who,
tell me how they are doing,
what they feel,
where they've been and how, I, appear to them.
They never ask if I am well, healthy or happy!
What DOES my friendship mean to you?

Does listening to me or caring about me matter?

When alone, I ask myself,
"Why do I feel angry and out of sorts?"
After realizing my ears have been accosted,
my attention demanded,
my generosity taken for granted,
my time usurped and energy invaded –
I ask myself,
"WHAT DOES MY FRIENDSHIP MEAN TO ME?"

As Hillel's heiress, my inheritance is
 "If I am not for myself, who will be for me?"

Being for myself IS being for you.

When I am ONLY for you,
I am not for me.

It is then I ask myself,
"How can my friendship mean anything
to you if it means nothing to me?"

When the World Is On Fire

When the world is on fire
do you close your eyes? Ignore it?
Do you?

Fuelled by racial discrimination
this conflagration
is a spirit abomination
this IS my nation
home of my education
playground of my indoctrination
to a world of justification
looking for integration
knowing that communication
is the way forward

I say I want a revolution, a human revolution
it's gonna have to start with me
the only solution for this revolution
Has to start with me

We're all in the same war
but not all in the same trenches
these flames are deep, embedded
we need more than hammers and wrenches

reformation, inner reformation
takes transformation
no longer subjugation
seeing ourselves as real

coexistence
human transformation
my own revolution
lighting my way and seeing you

Valiant Hummingbird

freely adapted from a story as told by Wangari Maathai

In a land far away
in a time not so long ago,
trees, animals, people lived peacefully side by side.

One night, or maybe it was day,
thunder boomed and lightning flashed.
One little spark flew onto a dry tree branch
and grew into a fire. The flame then became an inferno.
Tree, frond, grass, straw, wood, flowers,
everything was lapped up by the tongue of the fire.
The animals smelled smoke and started to run.
They ran fast and as far away from the heat as they could.
At the edge of the jungle/forest they turned, all of them –
and stopped.
The lions, elephants, monkeys and lemurs,
and all the other animal families,
just stopped, and stared at the flames engulfing their homes.
They stared and did nothing.

However, the little hummingbird fretted and flitted
and finally decided to fly to the nearest brook.
Taking a sip of water, the bird flew once more
gathering a sip of water in its long beak, then flew closer to the
flames.
The hummingbird let that little drop of water fall onto the flames.

All the other animals watching started to laugh,
mocking the efforts of the tiny little bird with the long beak.

"What good will one drop do?" cried the animals.
"Well," thought the hummingbird,
"the elephant could easily fill its large trunk with water
and hose the water onto the flames,
but the elephant did nothing,
just watched and waited and stared and stayed put!"

"Well," said the hummingbird,
"I'm doing the best I can
with or without a plan
flying with the wind in my wing
I can't flit around and do no thing
I have to take a stand and do some thing!!"

Shamed by the hummingbird's spirit of determination,
the elephant went to the brook and filled its trunk with water.
Then the elephant ambled towards the flames,
trying to douse the fire.
The others, likewise, were inspired to do something.
Thus, they began to help. Some kicked dirt at the fire.
Others brought drops of water.
When the conflagration was over,
the jungle/forest was burnt to the ground.

Again the hummingbird and the others did their part.
Seed by seed they replanted the earth.
Some birds dropped seeds from their beaks.
Some animals ate what little foliage they could find
and spit out the seeds.
Some animals foraged for seeds and carried them
in their mouths or on their skin or between their toes
and replanted the burnt out jungle/forest.

They worked tirelessly, companionably and with determination
until a whole world of cooperation was planted anew.

POEMS FOR YOU

CARNATION – The Variable Colour of Human Flesh

Dedicated to my beloved Mother, Yocheved Eva Novick, of blessed memory

Between the hours of the wolf and the snake,
in the midst of a dark, hot night, on the eve of
Friday the 13th, August, 1982, I shivered….
Through the heat, humidity, dust and sweat,
a cold, gossamer-like vapour filled the room.
It appeared as a ghost; a flying "skull-comet';
a spiritual messenger from the Angel of Death.
I shivered…. I knew…I was being forewarned…
Breathe deep…Don't get scared…Pay attention….
keep saying "I love you" like a mantra, over and over.
In the hot, summer night I shivered.
The portentous message was clear - My mother
was leaving. There are lines, like ties, that bind.
The Queen Streetcar is one of those lines.
It carried me from my studio to my mother's bed.
Bindings tie one generation to another.
Streetcar tracks transported my being to what was
left of my mother – her body, her image,
her slow, dying, breath. Heeding the message
of the cold vapour, I said, "I love you"
as tears spilled from my eyes. I said, "Thank you
for my life and my big brown eyes". I couldn't say
"Good bye"…Just come back soon, strong, healthy.

Ben Shmonim L'Gvurah*, Irving
A Tribute to Irving Layton**

Ben Shmonim l'gvurah, Irving.
Eighty is for strength.
Just keep on doing what you're doing.
Just keep on, keep on going.

My spirit-wings take me to a place
Where everyone's blest***
Where poems become songs
And songs become prayers
And the eternal is revered.

You are the definitive poet
Giving all you have
You set the classic standard
For this humble song of praise.

It is in being born that there is suffering.
And, as for growing older, the reward lies in wisdom.
Through the lesson of illness, the "truth-seeking-spirit" develops
But, birth and death alone, teach
The commonality of all humans.

So, take my hand in friendship.
Let's sing SHIR HAMAALOT****
It is an offering of grace,
A gift of a transcending soul.

Ben Shmonim l'gvurah, Irving,
Eighty is for strength.
Just keep on doing what you're doing,
Just keep on, keep on going.

*   a birthday greeting, Hebrew, literally means, "Son of 80 years,
have strength"
** Performed for Irving Layton at Centaur Theatre, Montreal
(with Leonard Cohen in attendance)
*** blessed
****The Psalms of David, Hebrew meaning "Songs of Ascent"

Norval Morrisseau,
A Brief Encounter, an Eternal Transformation *

It was just a brief, chance encounter many years ago, 1970s Toronto, maybe on
Queen St. West. I had been an original member of the iconic Canadian performance art group, "General Idea". I also worked with the Ontario Metis and Non-Status Indian Association (now defunct). Norval was already a legend, ephemeral, ethereal. If you didn't know who he was, you never would have known by his unassuming way.

I'll never forget meeting Norval. His spirit lives in the way I look at the lines of his paintings, his colours, his stories, his vision, his experience in this and other lifetimes. Each line is deliberate, intentional, unending, multi-layered, and meaningful.

When Norval died, on a grey autumn afternoon, I was compelled to pay my respects, go to the viewing at the funeral home. I needed to say "Meegwetch, Ahaam, So Long, Be well until next time, Journey Safely".

While standing over the coffin looking at Norval's body, I re-ceived a telephone call.
My friend and spirit sister, Cree Elder Pauline Shirt, called to ask me to sing "Amazing Grace" at Norval's funeral. She was the traditional native officiate. What a great honour!!!!

Of course I agreed and my heart started beating wildly because I didn't know his family, nor they me, however, I really trust Pauline.

When I called Pauline to inform her that I was writing this memory, she told me to offer tobacco to our Earth Mother and the Creator and ask Norval's spirit for a message.

I offered tobacco on the banks of a small river in the Hockley Valley. The sunset that evening was a huge, perfect ball of the brightest, blazing orange sinking into a black sky.
These colours are the voice of Norval. The perfect sunset is the eternal vision of life's breath.

Norval Morrisseau's gift to my world opened the door of my imagination to the astral plane, a world he knew but I didn't.

When the long lines filing past Norval's casket came dwindling to a few people lingering, it was time to sing. I really didn't feel "Amazing Grace' was the most fitting song. I publicly asked those at the funeral if I could sing an original song, "Adio Querido", rather than Amazing Grace. The melody is of the Ladino Jewish people with words written by me, words that say…
"goodbye my dear, I am so happy to know you, you have enriched my life
Your mother, when she brought you into the light, gave you a heart that loves much… Now you seek other flames, now you knock on other doors, now you light other passions, but to me, you LIVE! "…

I sang for the Morrisseau family- daughter, sons and brother. Norval's brother said,
"I didn't want the song to end". Me, too! As the Inuit say, "Songs are thoughts".
For Norval Morrisseau, ideas are songs, songs are gifts, gifts are colours, and stories, people and creatures and all living beings

*published by McMichael Canadian Art Museum's website

From "Bheir Me Oh" –The Timeless Air of Friendship

We are woven together by many songs,
mostly nonsense syllables, vocalese, if you please,
vocables or tra la lees.
And then there's "Bheir Me Oh"
Scottish, Gallic, meaning— what you will.

I didn't know Mary very well but I could sing "Bheir Me Oh".
One clear day, out of the clear blue,
the phone rings and Mary says, "Next Tuesday morning,
at 10:00 a.m. I'm having my breast removed.
I'm nervous about the anesthesia.
Will you sing "Bheir Me Oh" at that time?
If anything happens to me, I'd like to think
that lullaby will carry me on to my next destination."

At 10:00 a.m., with tape recorder in hand,
I sat in the middle of my room and sang
"Bheir Me Oh Ho Ro Van Oh…." over and over.

The first half-hour passed,
still I continued, until
the invisible feeling of danger dissipated.

The breast that suckled her children,
filled her clothing,
experienced puberty,
womanhood and then disease, was gone,
surgically separated from her body.

With indomitable spirit she said,
"It's just my breast, not my life".
And from this breast, like the teat
that feeds the world's soul,
a profound friendship was woven
by the air of a beautiful, timeless, melody.

Nomads on The Silk Road – For Bai li

nomads on the Silk Road
slog onward
in a spring teeming with colour
en garde for every unforeseen danger
"Courage, Vision, Strength", their mantra
their aspirations tinted by a kinder pink
signal a change not readily welcomed

nomads on the Silk Road
sit under
the blossoming cherry tree
petals canopy each delicate dream
kiss a tenderness
conquer the fears of the unknowable
while maintaining balance between bravado and hope

down the way sits a blind man who really has vision
over there paces a man with a full belly
        in constant hunger
over that way a mute with a voice
        hidden in pantomime
there lounges a deaf man who hears only what he chooses
here stands a kind man who doesn't know
        where to go nor what decisions to make

nomads on the Silk Road
hold fast each other's hands
walk together
lean on one another

obliterate the futility of despair
don the lion's spirit
infuse the sun's courage
vanquish the moment's desolation

On display at the Richmond Culture Centre
Life Celebration of Bail Lik, Richmond B.C. 2010

For the Voiceless and AIDWYC (Association in Defense of the Wrongfully Convicted)

"I have to forgive him," says Bill,
"Or else anger might take over my life."(1)
When meeting him, Bill seemed "other" worldly,
infusing the historic Truscott press conference
with dignity and integrity.
Acquitted, Steven and the Truscott family left for home.
AIDWYC's lawyers, staff, volunteers, friends
and Bill went to lunch.

I shared hummus (mashed chick peas, tahini,
lemon, garlic) and triangles of pita bread.
Bill had never heard of nor tasted this food.
It was a tender moment in a new experience
offered to this man who spent 12 years in a prison
wrongfully accused, tried and wrongfully convicted!
With the fortunes of fate, circumstances and good will
he was released, eventually acquitted, exonerated.
Thus, he sat next to me and we ate.
.

The sun's light truly shone in radiance and in essence.
That day tears cooled the intense sadness of injustice,
just as punctuation marks, grace notes and spice,
add rhythm, tone and flavour to a creation,
and like a creation, the mystical fingers of
the unknowable brought me to this place.

One witness' authorized, sanctioned,
erroneous expertise caused more grief
to more people than can be counted.
Yet, still, we are taught not to question authority.
If we, as a society, are not enraged,
we are not paying attention!

In time the world would hear
William Mullins-Johnson say,
"Forgiving somebody, and wanting somebody
to be held accountable are two different things". (2)

We, as a society, must be held accountable
to a higher standard of being so that
we, as a society, can greet a new chapter
in a new beginning of lives forth giving.

CODA (From my conversation with Bill)

How did you keep the beating of the drum?
How did you honour the rising of the sun?
How deep did the loneliness try to wear you down?
How did you win and stand to fight another round?
I LISTENED!
I listened to my heart as it kept to the beating of the drum.
I listened to the energy in the rising of the sun.
I listened to the loneliness and fought to win another round.

(1) and (2) are printed, in black on white, in MacLean's Magazine (Feb. 2008)

Let's Talk About The Realm of Possibility

dedicated to all the children who didn't come to life through my body, yet wound up in my arms, close to my heart

It is possible to hear your own thoughts
It is possible to touch the sky
It is possible to feel the depths of your own heart
It is possible to see the sun shining and to believe
that what we want is what we really see

It is possible to discover the fountain of youth exists within our
own aging body
It is possible to discover that eternity exists even in the face of
death
It is possible to discover that we can love our enemy without
being their friend
It is possible to believe that what we see exists in what we really
want

It is possible to experience infinite love while swimming
through a pool of sorrow

The Realm of Possibilities will embrace you
Are you open to accept it?
Letting go of all that binds us to the past
is the most difficult task of all, yet
it is as simple as
opening and closing the palm of your hand

It is possible to wake up in the morning and see the sun
beyond the clouds

It is possible to know each human being lives
in the image we see reflected in the mirror

OH, MOTHER EARTH (song lyric)

CHORUS: OH, MOTHER EARTH, WE ARE YOUR CHIL-
DREN
TREES'N'PEOPLE'N'FIELD'N'STREAM
OH, MOTHER EARTH, WE ARE YOUR CHIL-
DREN
WE WANT TO THANK YOU, WE WANT TO
DREAM

Expediency lives in our hearts, just for a dollar, just for a buck
We rip off tomorrow, we sell off today
What makes us think we won't have to pay?

CHORUS

The trees give their lives to unmask people's greed
People and trees are all family
We're killing this planet by selling our mother

CHORUS

How can I be still and keep my mouth shut?
The air is polluted, the water is too.
Our time may be borrowed, our time may be through
We're selling our future by hating our mother

CHORUS

My cry is a warning the chaos is near,
We're killing our planet by bowing to fear

Can you hear me Mother Earth?
The love in my heart?
My laughter is hidden, my tears everflow

CHORUS

Our hearts they are breaking and need to be filled
This planet is family it musn't be killed

FINAL CHORUS

Oh, Mother Earth, We are your children
Trees'n'people'n'field'n'stream
Oh, Mother Earth, We are your children
We NEED to thank you, we NEED to dream.

THE CITY is for PEOPLE

In her introduction to "The Death and Life of Great American Cities",
Jane Jacobs says, "..please look closely at real cities. While you are
looking, you might as well listen, linger and think about what you see.."
The lyrics to this song are inspired by those words. The melody is very beautiful
and this song is dedicated to Jane Jacobs and her family.

The City is for People,
For you, for me, for who we want to be
Look, Listen, Linger,
Think about what you see

The City is about stories,
Yours, mine, what we want to hear
Look, Listen, Linger
Think about what you feel

Some are neighbours, friends,
Some are family
And for those like you who teach, help and inspire
We offer in grace,
This embrace

The City can be an oasis,
For you, for me

For where we want to dream
Look, Listen, Linger,
Think about what you see, dream, feel.

RED BIRD

(Written in a 4 minute exercise at L.D. Pettigrew's Writing Out Loud workshop, April 30, 2002)

I think of myself as a red bird, soaring high in the sky.
Not a robin or a cardinal, but a spirit bird who travels between real worlds and mythical worlds.
It never sleeps.
It is a witness.
It has no friends, no enemies, no family.
It is a spirit voice who takes on the mantle of a red bird.
Once, my friend M. Joe, who is an artist, sent me a small painting
    of a red bird soaring beyond the clouds into the blue skies.
I will never know how he chose to paint a red bird and associate that with me.
I sometimes wonder if I was a First Nations person in a former life and if
    that red bird is something I remember from those times.

Kintsugi - This One's For You

I will gather the bits of my fragmented thoughts
and somehow glue them together with gold
like the centuries old Japanese porcelain art form
Kintsugi

shards held together with flowing gold
making the cup different and better
and far more beautiful
flowing gold hardening
connecting each shard
forming new
touching the broken
loving it
knowing it has its own value

to be in the presence of such divinity
is to feel
is to be alive
is to care
is to ask to be cared for
is to be open to once again be broken

ROBESON and MURPHY of VANCOUVER

Union leader Ray Stevenson tells the story of Harvey Murphy,
and
PAUL ROBESON, grand basso, humanist, lawyer, football
player,
"negro", communist.
These two men (and others) made history in
a cultural exchange, a demonstration for peace
when in 1952, 40,000 Vancouverites, other B.C.ers
and Americans gatheredd for the Peace Arch Concert

Like a nugget hidden in the palm of the hand,
this story unfolds and proffers for history.
In another day and age, Harvey Murphy,
Union Director of Mine, Mill and Smelter Workers'
of British Columbia,
invites the great singer to address the 1952 union's convention.
But these were bleak times when beliefs and commitments
caused the American government to revoke Robeson's
passport, disallowing him to travel and work.
Says Murphy of Vancouver, "aware of the union's stand
with respect to their black members and other oppressed
people, Robeson readily accepted the invitation…"
Since no native-born American ever needed a passport
to enter Canada, no trouble was expected. Wrong!!!
Waiting were many Canadians and a very friendly
Vancouver press. Robeson was assured the government
of Canada would not refuse him entry.
Vancouver was waiting to give him a warm welcome.
However, the American State Department threatened

to imprison and fine him for singing!
While Robeson argued with the border guard,
a Union delegation arrived to escort him to Vancouver.
He wasn't allowed to enter Canada.
Delegate Murphy proposed Robeson sing
on one side of the border to an audience on the other side.
In time, an illegal electrical phone hook up was created.
Disappointed Union members assembled at the hall.
Unbeknownst to them, Robeson phoned.
Through loud speakers he addressed them and
vowed to come back singing.

Murphy drafted a resolution listing grievances against
the U.S. State Department and
determined to broadcast the incident widely by setting up a
concert,
May 18, 1952, at the Peace Arch in Blaine, Washington,
just over the American border.

To make the Robeson rally a gathering of
international significance for peace and freedom,
the union members set up an upright piano on a truck bed.
Speakers were arranged so that a large crowd could hear.
40,000 Canadians and Americans showed up!

From the heart of the Vancouver people, this historical
nugget attests to a grassroots legend born, instilling
pride in a viable, unforgettable, indomitable spirit!

A Sonnet for the Landscape
for Barb Nahweghabow

visiting our relations, the winged ones
the swimmers, those with roots, the 4-footed ones
compelled her to venture south to the lake
the water welcomes her, comforts her
    with solace, sound and movement
the rhythm of the water sings its strength
the majesty of the clouds make their presence known
she says hello to the preening swans,
    swimming ducks,flying gulls and a lone mink
running rampant on the rocks as people canoe
    these freezing waters
on the other side of the lake, a chickadee flies to her
singing "chickadee, chickadee dee dee'
winter in covid times has its beauty, wild senses enter the land-
scape
For International Women's Day - March 8

it seems some things never change
disappointing, but not strange
for instance, take the war waged on women
for our bodies, eggs, yolks and albumen

"you've come a long way, baby" isn't far enough
I'm sad to say,
because fifty or so years after that slogan's launch
it seems we still havent' gotten up off our own haunch

women, stalwart warrior women
deligent, vigilant and true
no one will pave the way for you
realize, internalize, recognize
you are your own hard-won prize

earn a degree, get a certificate, learn the value of the picket
create a league or join a union
find out where to meet your legions
stand up tall, voice dissent
dream about becoming president

humble huntress of the truth
embodiment of eternal youth
intrepid champions of the victory way
tomorrow's success is seeded today!!!

I Revel With Applause

I revel with applause.

Some people in the USA
understand for every effect
there was a cause
George Floyd you did not die in vain
the whole world not only feels but saw your pain

I revel with applause
the sanity of humanity still remains,
what does it take to value a person's life
would somebody please explain.

i can't understand those who don't feel we are all connected
maybe, one day, I pray 420 will be celebrated -
for honouring the herb
for trying to forget hitler born on this day
for remembering twelve people saw the truth
exercised their common sense
showed the world there is no defense
for hatred, that will only incense
a world craving a better lens
to a compassionate humanity
the only way to cleanse this depravity
is to find guilty someone who thought he could kill
and not be punished.
There is a difference between justice
and being held accountable and for that

I revel with applause

Our Beloved High Park

How wonderful it was for immigrants just to get on the College Street streetcar travelling all the way westbound into High Park, the municipal garden refuge of these newly-arrived people with or without money. Here on this land, all 398 acres of it, on the traditional and ancestral lands of the Mississaugas of the Anishinaabe, the Haudenosaunee Confederacy, the Huron-Wendat and Petun Nation, people could relax in the verdant greenery, enjoy fresh air in the big city, play ball on the grass, have a picnic, fish in Grenadier Pond, walk along the paths leading to the water, Hillside Gardens overlooking the Maple Leaf Garden or the zoo. Here, our beloved High Park beckoned all to its oasis.

I sing your praises,High Park, once owned by Mr. Howard, given your name because of the height of the hill overlooking Humber Bay and Lake Ontario. The hippies had other connotations. What's in a name? During the 1960s and early 1970s, during the cultural revolution, High Park was accessible, a go-to place for dancing on the grass, daring to smoke it under the sun and feeling groovy and high even though it was illegal then and park police patrolled the land often.

I sing your praises, my beloved High Park because as a child, going to your zoo-penned animals gave insight to other species and how they lived. As a little girl I could go up to the fence containing bison and actually pick off a piece of bison "fur". It was an unusual experience that I would only share with the bison as the adults thought "ugh" why would she want to do that. I just wanted to bond with a buffalo. I can still feel its texture in my mind's memory.

I don't know when I actually began to be uncomfortable in the zoo-looking at the animals far away from their natural habitat but I still loved going to the park.

After my beloved mother passed, my father and I drove into the park. We would go to the restaurant. Mainly we would go near Grenadier Pond and sit and remember my mother there. One afternoon, I had a toothache. I asked my father for $70.00 for the dentist. He wouldn't give it to me. Nothing I could do about that. High Park had other ideas. (He really was a very nice person but had issues and some of those issues had to do with not having money). As we drove home, me in the driver's seat, I saw some coloured paper on the ground. I stopped the car, got out and found three twenties and one ten on the road. Astonished at this "miracle" I smugly looked at my father, grateful that my beloved High Park was taking care of me. I still wonder how that money got there.

Over the years High Park became a sort of pilgrimage. Cherry blossoms fell, flitted and free-flowed like snowflakes in the special Cherry Blossom grove. These are the descendents of the initial gift of 2000 cherry trees from the Japanaese ambassador on April 1, 1959. They were the gesture of appreciation from the citizens of Tokyo to the citizens of Toronto for accepting to re-locate Japanese Canadians after World Ward II. When the blossoms are in full mode to drop, the air becomes white with petals and the hillside becomes a wonderland of people and petals dancing, taking photos being enthralled.

There is a children's garden running southbound from the restaurant where a straw-bale house now sits and where children could come to learn about plants and herbs and how to cook and how the soil nourishes us. One season they had a festival. They needed entertainment. I got the gig. I went to sing in the open air for the children. I was served a meal based on all that was grown there that season. I still have a relationship/friendship with one of the park's gardeners. The soil does that. It bonds friends to one another. When I took on the responsibility of teaching a young woman who was quadriplegic, to sing, I took her to the children's garden . She loved High Park. The paved paths were easy for her wheelchair to traverse. The air refreshed her and the rhythm of the silence, even amongst all the people strolling in the park was calming. There are always lots of people in our beloved High Park.

There are festivals and sports and Shakespeare in the Park and the Scream in the Park but I created a tribute to National Poetry Month by having an outdoor poetry festival overlooking the still, cold, deep waters of Grenadier Pond. Bill bissett read as did Joan Sutcliffe. Director Ruth Ruth Stackhouse came to support . We stopped people walking by inviting them to enjoy poetry by local poets. In time, we would name our poetry group "The High Park Poets" because our beloved High Park evokes inspiration.

There is a spiritual labyrinth in the park. People come to walk in meditative thought. I went once with Joan and was given a gift only High Park could give. That year, the captivating monarch butterflies were threatened with extinction. People everywhere did their best to keep the butterflies alive. They planted milkweed and stopped spraying. As I sat relaxing after my meditative walk, a monarch butterfly appeared in the bushes. That gave me hope.

Once again our beloved High Park did its magic. It uplifted my spirits showing me that beauty is real, especially in the midst of a big bustling city. It taught me that there is more to be seen than what can be seen with the naked eye. It reminded me to respect this sacred native land. It helped keep my spirits resilient and optimistic. It strengthened me, my inner me. This is my beloved High Park. This is our beloved High Park.

My Mother, the SABRA

My Mother, a proud Israeli
was called a "Sabra"
"Sabra" means prickly pear, cactus fruit
An appropriate metaphor
for one thorny on the outside
numerous seeds inside and
sweet and juicy beyond imagining

I loved my mother just as I love this fruit
and found it interesting, coincidentally
they are equally difficult to reach

At age eleven, my mother and I went to Israel
without my father
His work denied him time off, he needed to earn money

after 36 years, 3 wars and much longing
 my mother went to Israel to re-unite with her sister

This new world was an education in itself
This foreign language was spoken rapidly, gutturally
Contexts and experiences alien until
I was enticed to go picking Sabras

Method: Find tin can, unwind metal hanger
Wind then fasten hanger with a long stick onto tin can,
Protect arms, legs and eyes from thorns
enter cactus grove

At first I dithered, scared and unfocussed
But once I determined to focus, I extended my arm,
coordinated it with can and aimed for fruit

Carefully placing apparatus onto desired fruit
I jiggled that fruit, a lot, till one after another pear
fell into can and carefully, tenderly
placed in basket, exited grove carefully

with gloved hands, pick up fruit
cut ends of thorny skin, slide knife down the middle
remove frutiy pulp, bite, let juice drip down chin
fall in love, fly to heaven, devote oneself to
loving the cactus prickly pear

This was the methodogy of dealing with my mother,
approach with caution, protect myself,
empathize with her needs
(this daughter of a prickly pear was becoming skilled at survival)
use guile to manipulate, focus, become stubborn
get reward, express love, undying forever love
yet under that rough exterior was such sweetness
such goodness
just like the cactus pear reward
True love, eternally

Writing Out of My Own Horn

"Music is your own experience, your thoughts, your wisdom.

If you don't live it, it won't come out of your horn."

Charlie Parker

Singing has been my first love. When I wanted to sing words that meant something to me, I sought those words of meaning. If and when I couldn't find them, I started to write my own singable words.

I came to writing later in life. It was very personal, like being with a lover, yearning for my mother or father's comforting shoulder or just having a friend. Poetry was and is the most accessible. I can distill my feelings and observations into poetic expressions. I could conquer the devil of loneliness and squelch the fire of the raging dragon. Most importantly, writing helps me make new friends. Not always, as some people don't always agree with my point of view but I always challenge myself to hope my writing could connect with you, the reader. Would you be interested in seeing me, knowing me as a friend, neighbour, citizen? Are there various ways I can capture your attention and engage your interest?

As a teenager in the exciting 1960s, I was inspired by Anne Frank to keep a diary and did so consistently for 9 years. Mainly I wrote about how I wanted to sing. In retrospect, I was writing about wanting to be heard. Slowly that started to happen. In time, I became the singer who could interpret poetry and sang tributes to Irving Layton, Leonard Cohen, bill bissett, Austin Clarke, George Elliott Clarke, Bob Dylan and many others. Through the voices of others, I found my own sound, color, authenticity (a journey that is constantly evolving).

It takes courage, a sense of imaginative adventure and a desire to want to be heard through the pen, the horn, the voice. It must be done. How else can humanity survive, if we don't reach out to one another at the cost of seeming foolish? Let's all fly by the seat of our pants or the slits in our skirts and soar in this unlimited realm of using the word as the lamp that lights the way. After all, in a darkened cave, when one lights a match, everything is illuminated.

"We can easily forgive a child who is afraid of the dark; the real tragedy of life is when people are afraid of the light!"   *Plato*

published in The Writer's Union of Canada magazine "Write" Vol 49, No. 1, Spring 20201

Thank you to all who read and who read this manuscript.

With special thank yous to Professor Evelyn Marrast, Joan Sutcliffe and Dr. John Clifton

www.ingramcontent.com/pod-product-compliance
Lightning Source LLC
LaVergne TN
LVHW051448170726
843492LV00002B/588